STEP-by-STEP
GEOGRAPHY

Seas and Coasts

Patience Coster

Illustrated by Andrew Farmer
and Shirley Tourret

W
FRANKLIN WATTS
LONDON • NEW YORK • SYDNEY

© 1997 Franklin Watts

First published in Great Britain by
Franklin Watts
96 Leonard Street
London
EC2A 4RH

Franklin Watts Australia
14 Mars Road
Lane Cove
NSW 2006
Australia

ISBN: 0 7496 2611 9
10 9 8 7 6 5 4 3 2 1
Dewey Decimal Classification 551.4
A CIP catalogue record for this book is available from the British Library

Printed in Dubai

Planning and production by The Creative Publishing Company
Design: Ian Winton
Consultant: Keith Lye

The publishers would like to thank The Royal Life Saving Society UK for their assistance.

Photographs: Bruce Coleman: page 9 (Luiz Claudio Marigo), page 19,
bottom (G Ziesler), page 24 (Luiz Claudio Marigo); James Davis: cover; Robert Harding Picture
Library: page 5, bottom (Adina Tovy), page 11 (Jackie Dunn), page 27, bottom (Gary Williams);
Image Bank: page 31 (Jeff Hunter); Oxford Scientific Films: page 19, top (Harold Taylor), page 20
(Laurence Gould), page 22 (Peter Parks); Tony Stone Worldwide: page 5, top (Graeme Norways),
page 7 (Shaun Egan), page 13 (James Randklev), page 23 (Norbert Wu), page 26 (Glen Allison), page
27, top (Kevin Cullimore), page 30, top (Peter Cade), page 30, bottom (David Woodfall).

Contents

The Seaside

Have you ever visited the seaside?
What did you do there? Did you
build sandcastles, explore rock
pools, go for a swim?

The seaside is where the land
meets the sea. It is a special
place, with breaking waves,
caves and sand dunes, seaweed,
shellfish and sea birds.

Another name for the seaside is the coast. There are different kinds of coast all over the world. Some are rocky with few trees.

Other coasts have long sandy beaches and palm trees.

5

What Are Tides?

Did you know that the level of the sea rises and falls? This happens about twice every day. When the level of the sea rises it is called high tide, when it falls this is low tide.

At high tide, the beach is mostly covered by the sea. At low tide, the sea is sometimes far away and there is a large area of wet sand to play on.

As the tide goes out, seaweed, driftwood and other **debris** are often left in a line on the beach. This line is the high tide mark.

What Lives on the Seashore?

Different areas of the shore have different types of wildlife. Sea birds gather on wide, sandy beaches. Rocky parts of the shore may have lots of pools that are home to many animals.

Limpets, mussels, crabs and shrimps live in rocky pools. The seaweeds in and around these pools shade them from the sun.

In pools nearer to the sea there are sea anemones, starfish, sea urchins and small fish.

Small animals can hide under seaweeds from **predators** such as seagulls.

In some cold places, penguins live on the shoreline. In some hot countries, turtles come ashore to lay their eggs.

On sandy beaches most of the animals live in the mud beneath the sand.

Seagulls and wading birds feed on the many seashore animals.

Sandworms live in U-shaped burrows.

Shrimps and crabs wait in the mud for the sea to cover them before they come out to feed.

Cockles and razor-shells live in the mud.

Waves

Have you noticed how waves ruffle the surface of the sea? These waves are caused by the wind.

A light breeze makes small ripples. A **moderate** wind can cause steep waves. A strong wind will build very high waves indeed.

Giant Waves

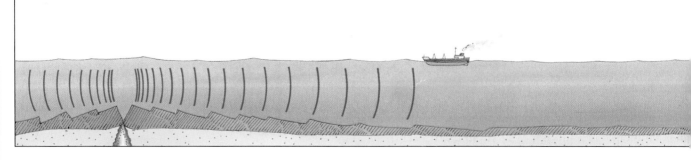

The biggest waves of all are not made by the wind. They are caused by earthquakes or volcanoes **erupting** under the sea.

In many parts of the world, people like to surf these high waves.

MAKING WAVES

1 Fill a tank with water. The bigger the tank, the bigger the waves will be.

2 Blow across the water in the tank. First blow hard and then blow gently. Even if you blow very gently you will still make some waves.

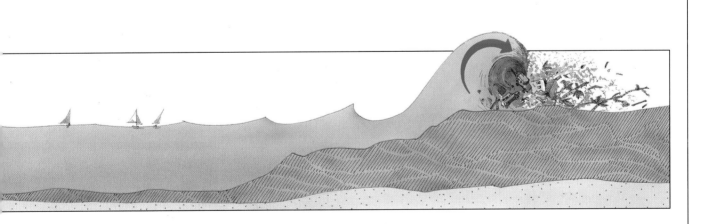

These giant waves are called **tsunamis**. Some tsunamis are more than 60 metres high. They can flood low-lying coasts and drown thousands of people.

Cliffs and Rocks

Coastlines are always slowly changing. In some places, the sea wears away the land. Waves pick up sand and pebbles and hurl them at the shore. The pounding waves open up cracks in the cliffs which are gradually hollowed out into caves.

Always ask an adult before exploring caves and cliffs.

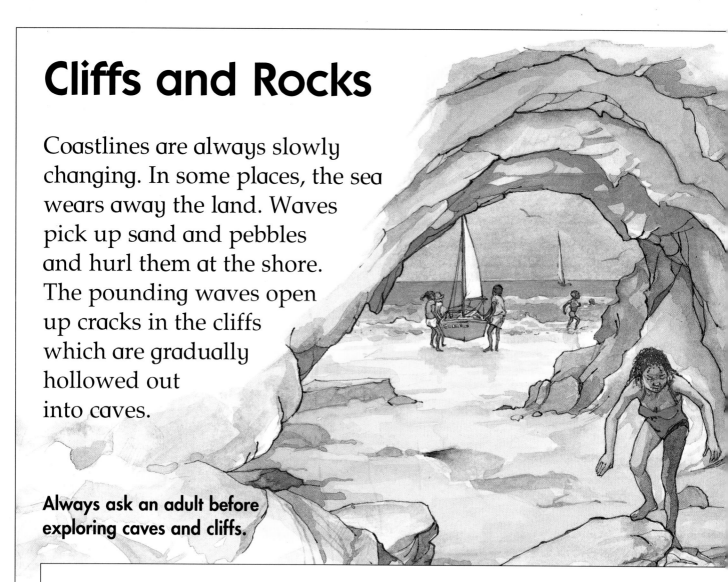

How Stacks Are Formed

Waves beat against the cliffs, wearing them away.

Slowly, caves form on either side of the **headland**.

Huge chunks of rock break off and fall into the sea. Here the waves break the rocks into more pebbles.

Lighthouses warn ships that they are near a rocky coast.

The caves are worn away until they meet and make an arch.

The roof of the arch collapses, leaving a stack.

Beaches and Dunes

Along some coasts, the action of the sea builds
up land instead of wearing it away.

Waves dump bits of rock on the shore.
The rocks may be very large or they
may be small pebbles, worn smooth
from being rubbed together by the sea.

A bar is a long, narrow mound
of sand and pebbles off-shore.

These mudflats have been
made by the river dumping its
load as it flows into the sea.

Winds blowing on to the
shore may build sand into hills,
called dunes. Sea grasses and other plants
may grow in the sand and help to hold the dunes in place.

Sand is made up of tiny grains of rock and shells that have been pounded by the sea. Beaches are built up when waves dump sand on the shore. Other fine material called **silt** is dumped by rivers where they flow into the sea.

A spit is a long, narrow beach joined to the land at one end.

Rivers carry tiny amounts of salt from the land to the sea. Over millions of years this has made the sea water salty.

A Watery Planet

Much of the Earth is covered with salt water. This water fills huge dips in the Earth's surface to form oceans and seas. The largest of these are the Pacific, Atlantic, Indian and Arctic oceans.

The Marianas Trench

The deepest point of all the oceans is the Marianas Trench in the Pacific. Here Mount Everest could be buried without trace.

ARCTIC OCEAN

NORTH AMERICA

PACIFIC OCEAN

AUSTRALIA

The Pacific is the biggest ocean. All the dry land on Earth could fit into it. It is also the deepest ocean, plunging to 11 kilometres at the Marianas Trench.

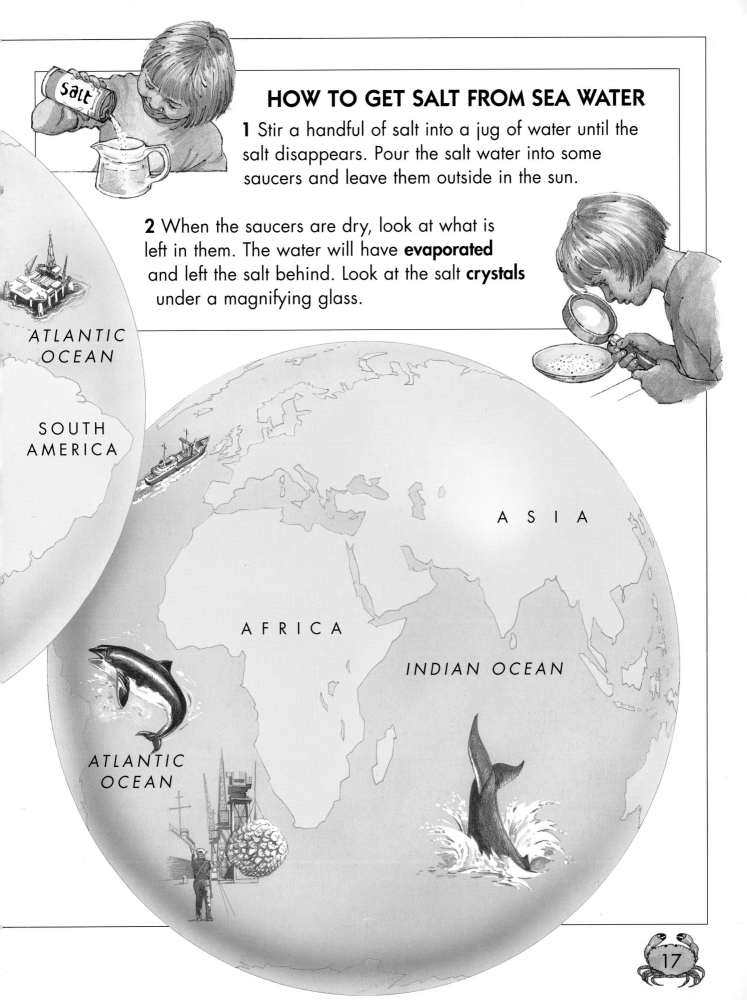

HOW TO GET SALT FROM SEA WATER

1 Stir a handful of salt into a jug of water until the salt disappears. Pour the salt water into some saucers and leave them outside in the sun.

2 When the saucers are dry, look at what is left in them. The water will have **evaporated** and left the salt behind. Look at the salt **crystals** under a magnifying glass.

ATLANTIC OCEAN

SOUTH AMERICA

ASIA

AFRICA

INDIAN OCEAN

ATLANTIC OCEAN

The Surging Sea

The waters of the oceans are always moving. Much of this movement is caused by currents. These are streams of water in the ocean that flow in a certain direction.

Near to land there are coastal currents caused by tides and waves. On beaches where strong currents flow near the shore, you may see red flags and signs warning that swimming is dangerous.

There are much greater currents out in the ocean. Ocean currents affect the weather on land. Warm currents help to keep the weather in coastal areas warm, cold currents keep it cold.

Rivers in the Ocean

Ocean currents carry plant and animal life far and wide. These coconuts are sprouting into new plants. The tree from which they fell is on another beach far away.

Some sea animals, like whales and porpoises, travel long distances with the help of ocean currents.

A Secret World

At the edge of each **continent** the land slopes gently down under the sea. This is the continental shelf.

How would you like to travel to the bottom of the sea? You would see an amazing landscape there, normally hidden from view.

Studying Shipwrecks

Divers explore the wrecks of ships that sank long ago. These give us a good idea of what life was like then.

Beyond the continental shelf the **ocean floor** may plunge down steeply to a deep trench.

Deep sea exploration is carried out by submersibles. These underwater craft may be operated by a person inside, or they may be **remote-controlled**.

Scientists use ships equipped with special tools and instruments to tell how deep the sea is and take samples from the ocean floor.

Great mountains, valleys and plains make up the ocean floor. In some places mountains break through the surface of the ocean to form islands.

Submersibles are sent down to map these great ocean trenches.

MAKE A SUBMARINE

1 Fix a small piece of Plasticine to the bottom of a pen top. Alter the amount of Plasticine so that the top just floats in water. Drop the pen top into a plastic bottle three-quarters filled with water. Screw the lid on.

2 Squeeze the bottle. The pen top will sink to the bottom. Release the bottle and it will rise to the surface again. In a similar way, water is let into empty chambers on board a submarine when it needs to dive.

What Lives in the Sea?

Plant and animal life in the sea changes the deeper you go. There are lots of animals near the surface, but in the dark depths the animals are far fewer, and much stranger looking!

At the surface, there are floating animals like jellyfish.

Near the surface where there is plenty of light the ocean is crowded with fish and their predators, such as sharks.

Deeper down there is a dimly-lit world. Lantern fish and hatchet fish live here.

Sea Food

Plankton are tiny plants and animals living in the ocean. They are so small that they can only be seen through a **microscope**. The fish and shellfish that eat plankton are in turn eaten by bigger fish and by birds and seals.

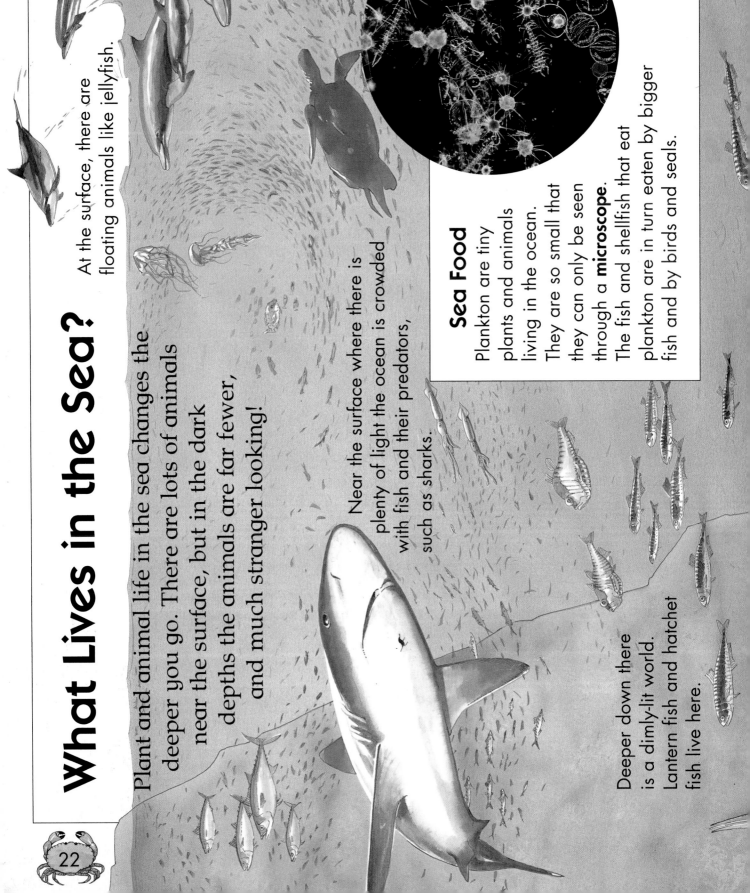

Deeper still there is very little light. Gulper eels swim with their large mouths open to catch what prey they can.

This deep-sea angler fish draws its **prey** towards its waiting jaws with a special lure.

In the deepest parts of the ocean there is no light at all. Brittle starfish, tripod fish and sea cucumbers live on the ocean floor.

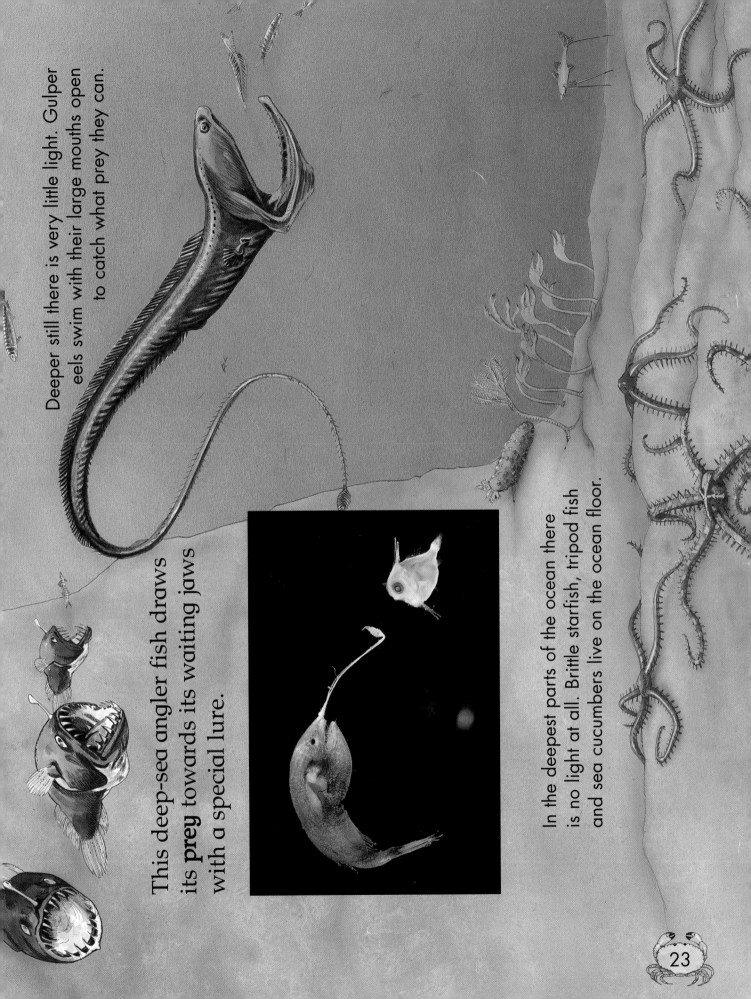

People and the Sea

People have fished the seas around the world's coasts for thousands of years. The first boats were simple rafts and hollowed-out canoes. Boats like this are still used in many parts of the world.

Long ago, people travelled the seas to find new lands to live in and for trade. They brought back gold, silver, precious stones, silk and spices. They made a lot of money selling these goods. They set up trading posts on the coasts of lands they visited.

Later, people began
to sail around the coasts of
lands in order to make maps.

Life by the Sea

Most of the world's people live on or near its coasts. Many large and prosperous cities have grown up along the ocean. This photo shows San Francisco, a bustling city on the Pacific coast of the United States.

Today's huge ports were originally stopping off places for shipping and for trade. People settled there when they saw that a living could be made from the sea.

People like to take their holidays by the sea, especially where the climate is good. They enjoy resting on the beach, sailing, swimming and **scuba-diving**.

In the event of storms, however, life by the sea can be dangerous.

Using the Sea

We use the sea in many ways. It is a rich source of food and other **resources**.

All over the world, boats search the oceans for fish.

People drill for oil and gas buried in rocks deep below the ocean.

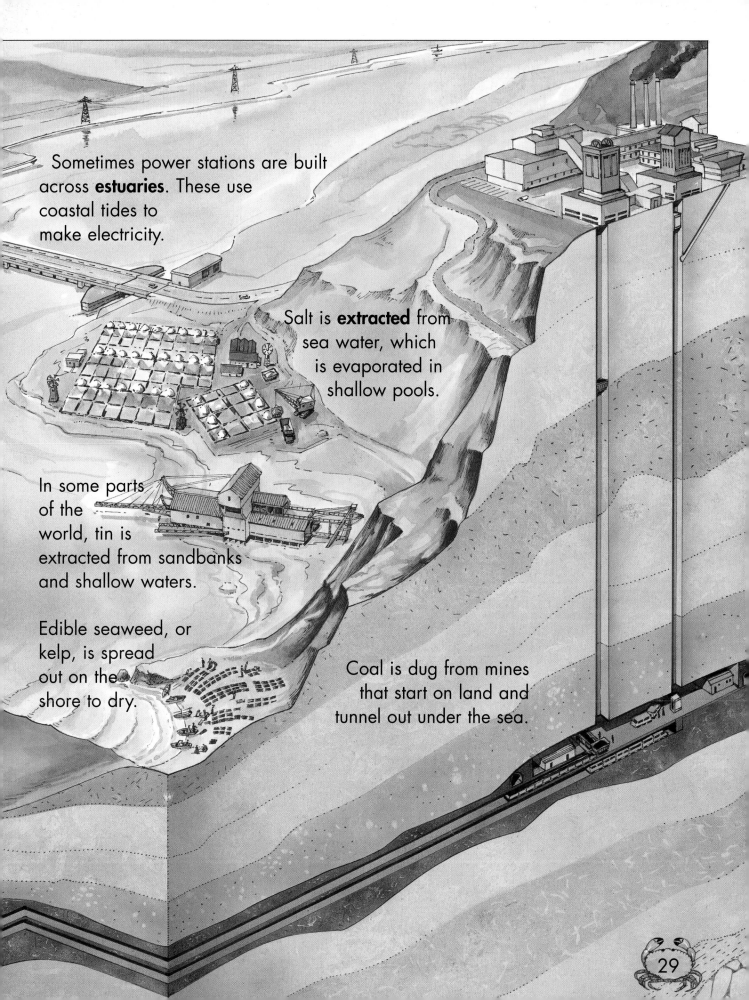

Sometimes power stations are built across **estuaries**. These use coastal tides to make electricity.

Salt is **extracted** from sea water, which is evaporated in shallow pools.

In some parts of the world, tin is extracted from sandbanks and shallow waters.

Edible seaweed, or kelp, is spread out on the shore to dry.

Coal is dug from mines that start on land and tunnel out under the sea.

Seas and Coasts in Danger

We do not always look after the world's seas and coasts. We dump rubbish, **sewage** and chemicals in the water. These things poison the seas and coastlines, killing plants and animals.

We take too many fish from the sea. This means that some kinds of fish are growing rarer.

If tankers carrying oil are damaged at sea, the oil spills out. It kills wildlife and **pollutes** the coasts.

Unless we limit what we dump in or near the sea, huge numbers of living things will continue to die.

Ravishing Reefs

In warmer parts of the world there are coral reefs, rich in wildlife. Reefs can easily be damaged by pollution. Some countries are now starting to protect these beautiful places.

Glossary

Continent: One of Earth's main large land areas

Crystals: Solid substances with a regular shape

Debris: Bits and pieces of rubbish

Erupting: Breaking out

Estuary: The wide mouth of a river, where it runs into the sea

Evaporate: To change into vapour

Extracted: Taken out

Headland: A point of land reaching out into the sea

Microscope: An instrument for magnifying very small objects

Moderate: Of medium strength

Ocean floor: The bottom of the sea

Pollute: To make dirty or harmful to human, animal or plant life

Predators: Animals that live by capturing and feeding upon other animals

Prey: An animal hunted for food by another animal

Remote-controlled: Controlled from a distance

Resources: Raw materials that can be used by people

Scuba-diving: Swimming and exploring underwater using scuba (self-contained underwater breathing apparatus) equipment

Sewage: Waste matter produced by people

Silt: Part of a river's load, made up of grains smaller than sand but larger than clay

Tsunamis: Giant waves caused by eruptions on the sea bed

Index